Does Anybody Else Hurt This Bad . . . And Live?

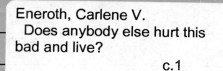

Eneroth, Carlene V.
 Does anybody else hurt this
bad and live?

c.1

Eneroth, Carlene V.
 Does anybody else hurt this
bad and live?

c.1

Does Anybody Else Hurt This Bad . . . And Live?

Carlene Vester Eneroth

Published by

Otis Publications

P.O. Box 6028

Spokane, WA 99207

Published by

Otis Publications
P.O. Box 6028
Spokane, WA 99207

Contact Otis Publications for information on quantity discounts.

Typesetting, Production and Cover Design by Byron King, Spokane, Washington

Second Printing - 1994

ISBN 0-9641637-0-5

Library of Congress Catalog Card Number: 94-092435

WE SALUTE

With love some special "survivors"
who know it hurts this bad . . .

• My priceless Mom, **Clara**, who recently lost **Carl**: her best friend and our
Dad;

• My terrific mother-in-law, **Clarice**,
who first lost **Lyall**, then my **Greg** and now,
little **Nate**;

and

• My "sounding board" and cherished
friend, **Ann Elise**, who lost her **Mike**.

HATS OFF TO:

Communication Resources,
P.O. Box 2625, North Canton, Ohio 44720
for their illustrations used by permission.

The writers, editors and publishers
who gave permission for quotations
from their copyrighted material.

and

Those who have willingly shared from their deep,
dark well of personal grief; and especially to my
support group called *Solitaires* (our definition: Even
though we stand alone, we can shine brilliantly like
a diamond solitaire and be attractive!). Names have
been changed here to protect their privacy.

TABLE OF CONTENTS

|URGENT!|

"I feel numb, like maybe it didn't really happen."

"It's so hard to hold it all in."

"I feel like a stuffed animal with its insides all pulled out."[1]

Sound familiar? Can you see yourself in each of these hodgepodge of emotions?? And you wonder . . .

Does anybody else hurt this bad . . . and live?

The funeral is over, some thank you's have been written but many others still remain; the mail brings more vague business forms and less of those welcomed sympathy cards; each day you awaken with the same awareness – someone you love is gone. It feels like someone ripped your heart out of your chest without an anesthetic!

Through all of this you're dismayed to discover you have no appetite; only total exhaustion. Meaningless days are followed by ceaseless nights.

Finally it dawns on you: "So <u>this</u> is grief! No matter how much I might have heard or read about it, even watched or helped others <u>in</u> it . . . **nobody** could ever have told me it would be like **this**." Is that how you feel? <u>Nobody</u> really understands what all of this grief business is like until it happens to them.

Although I can't know **exactly** how you feel, I have a fairly good idea what it's like when the whole world gets turned upside down in a few seconds. My husband, Greg, was 31 years old when he suffered a fatal heart attack in our water ski boat. After hearing the finality in the words "He's gone," I walked out of the Emergency Room, into the still brilliant sunshine of that hot August day. I was flabbergasted to see the sun still shining! How <u>could</u> it? Clearly, **my** world had just come to a screeching halt. Why would the universe remain unaltered??

As unbearable minutes and hours somehow turned into days and the weeks slowly gave way to months, it became impossible to convince me anyone else in this hemisphere could have hurt **this** bad . . . **and lived**. Definitely not!

It seemed to me the unwritten motto for the new survivor was,

When all else fails,
muddle through!

That's exactly what I did, of course. Was there another option? I found no magical pill to swallow which would eliminate my despair, of course. Yet I kept thinking, "There's <u>got</u> to be a better way to handle all of this!"

Maybe you are wondering <u>now</u>, as I did <u>then</u>, with so many "How To" books around for teaching the "ins and outs" of wallpapering, plumbing or home repair . . . why isn't there a "How To" list of tips to help me survive?

In the years following Greg's death, I was given the opportunity to conduct workshops and seminars on what we, as survivors, desperately wish our caring friends would do to help us. During this process, I happily discovered something: Many others who had walked this "Survival Road" ahead of me, had some ideas they were willing to share about their personal "How To's" in grief. Several of these ideas were the "potholes" to try and avoid, while others seemed designed to pave the bumpy gravel road ahead with practical tips.

Not wanting to keep all this splendid advise to myself, I have compiled here – just for you – many of these helpful hints. As you struggle to concentrate long enough just to get through these few pages (no small effort in itself!), I hope you'll find suggestions that make <u>your</u> walk (and sometimes crawl) along this Survival Road a little easier.

 Slowly ... <u>very</u> slowly ... you'll begin to notice you are moving ahead in your world of grief. May you then become aware of others who are hurting as you have been. And by finding the strength to care and share with them from the depth of your own experience, one day you'll be astonished to realize:

*"I <u>did</u> hurt this bad . . .
and I lived!"*

1

ARE YOU <u>SURE</u> THIS IS NORMAL?

Is there any such thing as normal any more? I longed for it . . . prayed for it . . . craved it. But if I couldn't go back in time where my life was normal (before grief so rudely intruded), could I at least know I was "doing grief" as normally as others before me?

Perhaps you feel that way too. If so, please read on . . .

Are you more exhausted than you've ever been in your entire life? Do you find that just getting out of bed in the morning uses up all your day's supply of energy? Or, maybe the course of least resistance is to just <u>stay</u> in that bed! I found I didn't even know the <u>meaning</u> of "tired" until I became an overnight survivor. Where in the world did all my stamina go? Why was I so lethargic . . . listless . . . and just plain "pooped?" For the longest time I believed it must be the result of one "whale" of a thyroid deficiency I'd suddenly acquired!

But a l o n g while later, when listening to Sharon, a Hospice Director, I heard her casually comment,

> *"Grief is the hardest work*
> *a person will ever do —*
> *harder than even digging*
> *ditches 12 hours a day."*

Stunned, I wanted to jump right out of my seat, grab her arm and yell, "Are you kidding? You mean I was normal to be dead tired every single day; that the biggest daily decision I could make was what breakfast cereal to put in my bowl? It was normal to fall into bed at 7 or 8 p.m. every single night, absolutely 'whipped?'"

It's impossible to describe what an astonishing relief that news was to me! It seemed I could (maybe) handle whatever was coming up in this business of grief . . . **if only I knew it was <u>normal!</u>**

Another thing driving me crazy was that just when I seemed to take even one tiny step forward in grief, I'd tumble backwards a half dozen steps. Shouldn't there be some steady progress I would notice? Surely everybody else <u>but</u> me must move ahead and not up and down like a little child's yo-yo.

For the longest time, every single day – every hour of each 24 – is just unmentionable. But then you might have a few good hours mixed in with the awful ones. At last, you begin to notice maybe a day or even two days, that are actually not <u>quite</u> as bad. Has the grief disappeared? Certainly not! But just having even one whole day where you have a spurt of energy and a few less tears is exciting. The problem comes that just when this happens (and when you least expect it!) grief sneaks up to run you down again. Because it's unexpected, you can't believe it's really happening.

Karen recalled she had been back to work for a few months and the day was going ok. She felt pretty much in control of her emotions that morning. Then a co-worker walked in with a plateful of peanut butter cookies to share. Those had been her son's favorites. She had to get up and walk away as it was such an unexpected reminder of something <u>else</u> he wouldn't ever be enjoying again. Something like that – so seemingly insignificant – turns the rest of the day instantly black. It's back on the grief treadmill again.

"Just the glimpse of an old black or navy blue Ford Ranchero will instantly do me in, on an otherwise halfway – decent day," shares Doyle. He went on to explain, "My son and I talked over his purchase of this kind of vehicle and after much consideration and taking Mom to check it out, we concluded this was the thing for him. Was he ever excited! It was such a big day in his life and in our father-son relationship. Since he's been gone, just seeing a vehicle like that, ruins the rest of my day."

Charlotte remarked that window shopping sometimes helped take her mind off her troubles. Walking through a new mall, she was enjoying a day away from home, temporarily escaping the loneliness she felt there. As she strolled through the drug store area, picking up some small necessities, she headed to the check-out stand. About to be waited on, her eyes fell on a sale rack of Tootsie Roll Pops . . . Gary's favorites. Those had been a "requirement" every year in his Christmas stocking. Even though they hadn't crossed her mind since his death, this one glance in the wrong direction put <u>her</u> back on that treadmill too. She barely got out of the store without bawling her eyes out.

Each of you has your <u>own</u> list of situations just like these, of course. It's such a vulnerable feeling to not know when another wave of grief will knock the stuffing out of you . . . again.

You know, before that August day on the lake, I kind of assumed those in grief would have their worst time the day of the funeral and then they could get better – a little at a time; kind of like having surgery. At first your stitches or staples hurt. You start off on clear broth and work your way up to poached eggs and finally solid food. At the start, you only swing your legs over the edge of the bed, but pretty soon, you're cautiously shuffling down the hall. Finally, you're on your way home. Sure: progress would sometimes appear slow but it <u>was</u> progress, just the same.

Isn't it a shock when grief turns out to be just the opposite of surgery? The day of the funeral is probably the best day you'll have in a very long time. Grief continues to get worse and worse, not better and better. As more of your numb brain thaws, the pain becomes increasingly unbearable. You can't remember your best friend's name, where you're headed when you get in the car, much less what to do if you <u>arrive</u> at that destination! It feels like an elephant is sitting on your chest, making it hard to even breathe.

Believe it or not, all of this too is quite normal and the list of grief symptoms continues.

Doesn't it drive you crazy when you just <u>have</u> to talk about your loved one and what happened to them but friends and family won't give you the chance? You want to repeat the circumstances of the death scene and have others feel the horror of what happened with you. But the subject is changed or you are "sshhed" and urged to go on to some other topic. Basically, that eliminated most of my conversation, that's for sure! There <u>was</u> nothing else I wanted to discuss.

Also, you desperately wish others would feel at ease bringing up your loved one's name in everyday conversation – especially as the months turn into years. Right? Ellie remarked:

> *"It just seems like everyone is trying to sweep him under the rug, like he didn't really exist. I know they mean well and think this helps me out but I wish they knew how I longed to*

hear his name again and know
someone was still thinking of him!"

When you're trying to hold back all the emotions and keep an outward appearance of "I can handle this" everyone assumes you really <u>are</u> doing fine! But just the opposite is true. One lady exclaimed:

"I have a newborn baby and a
recently dead husband and people
keep telling me 'You're doing so
well.' I want to say, 'Phone me at
midnight sometime and hear me
scream!'" [1]

Being in my 30's when Greg died, I assumed I wouldn't be having the kind of mental problems associated with grief in older folks. <u>They</u> would, surely, be the ones who would have difficulty with memory and concentration levels. Boy, was I wrong!

It was encouraging to hear that doctors say grief is such an incredible blow to our emotional and mental systems that the brain needs to shut down for brief periods of time to keep us from getting overloaded. That is some relief, isn't it? I found it took a gigantic mental effort on my part just to keep track of someone else's ordinary conversation. I simply could not concentrate on what they had to say. If it wasn't about grief, it was meaningless to me. Sitting down to read was close to impossible because the comprehension and retention of the written words was zero.

I recall receiving a nice little grief booklet the week Greg died. A few months later, I happened to find it in a dresser drawer, picked it up and read it through. In later mentioning this to my Mom, I watched as a look of astonishment came over her face . . .

"But dear, "she said, "you sat
down and read it through from cover
to cover the day after the
funeral. I saw you. Don't you
remember?"

Honestly, I had no recollection of that whatsoever! And as those things begin to happen you are positive you're headed for the "looney bin!"

Rest easy! All of these symptoms are common (and normal) to every single person in the midst of tremendous grief. Often, it helps to sit down and compare notes with other survivors, learning you're

not "The Lone Ranger" in feeling as you do.
During this stressful time,

Whatever you do . . . it's normal!
Almost anything goes!

YOU ARE NORMAL.

2

SLEEP . . .
WHERE IS IT?

"No matter <u>what</u> happens . . . nothing affects <u>my</u> sleep" I used to brag. Handling some disaster at work or during sad times with friends, people used to ask if I didn't have trouble getting to sleep over it. And that was what I'd always answer: "Heavens, NO! Nothing bothers my sleep!" But then Greg died and boy, did things change! Suddenly, even though I was absolutely dead on my feet all the time, I couldn't sleep but for a little bit at a time. I would fall asleep easily, that's true. Staying asleep? Never. I didn't know that this, too, was a common problem to survivors and so continued to be mystified that grief could bother even <u>this</u> area of my life.

It never occurred to my befuddled mind that you could look for ways to make sleep something easier to acquire . . . short of running a marathon or bawling until my eyelids were swollen shut! But I have since met creative people who used what little clarity of thought they had left, to come up with some ways that might help. Let's look at some of them:

I first met Tessa at a Grief Seminar last year. Two years before, she had lost her little boy and then last year, her husband died in her arms following an accident. (Now that's a double whammy!) Some of her methods for getting a little sleep included buying a set of lullaby tapes, such as the kind made for babies. She played them a lot at night, especially just before going to bed. They helped relax those tense muscles and taunt nerves. When these tapes didn't work their magic charm, she tried doing some exercises (such as sit-ups) for a few minutes. She went to the exercise routine even if it meant rising from bed at midnight – if sleep wouldn't come.

Other times, she found herself sitting up writing letters about how she felt. This relieved stress and also made her eyes tired. Many times she got out of bed to soak in a hot bubble bath to find relaxation and the subsequent sleep that had eluded her. (I just hear you fellows thinking, "Well, you won't catch me trying that bath idea! What would people think?!" However, I do know a man who does this very thing . . . soak in a hot tub in search of a few hours sleep.)

Exercise is a very real part of convincing our bodies they need sleep. It also helps to keep us slighty sane as well! Ellen said the health club membership she took out just after Mitch died, was an absolute priority item in her budget. Even though a couple of years have passed, she still makes time in her busy schedule for those necessary trips to the club.

Personally, I had absolutely <u>no</u> idea exercise could make me feel much better, let alone help me <u>sleep</u>. But one day, after sitting in my family room for what seemed like forever – bawling my head off, I thought, "Why don't you get up and try doing that simple exercise routine you used to work on?" You can imagine my level of enthusiasm for this little idea: none! But I finally said, "Oh why not?" I started in with the warm-ups that are done in grade school: reaching down with your fingertips to touch your toes. After doing this just a couple of times, my whole chest instantly felt lighter. I couldn't believe what was happening! That elephant sitting on my chest was shrinking! So I tried doing that more and more when I'd been crying nonstop and it really seemed to help. It was puzzling at first, when I realized that, not only did I feel better when exercising, but I slept better too. But then it dawned on me that even though I was always <u>mentally</u> exhausted, I had not been doing anything on a day-by-day basis to tire out my <u>physical</u> being!

Rachel, a young mother left with three small children, was surprised to notice her body chemistry used to be almost timed to the day of the month that her husband died. She would wake up feeling crummy, depressed and just plain "blah", only to glance at the calendar and realize it was another month date since Bill had died. Her solution?

> *"I go out to the living room and tell the kids they'll have to skip cartoons today because I have to turn the channel to the exercise show and work out. It's the best way I've found to help me get rid of the 'yuckies' on days like that."*

Obviously, it isn't practical for all of you to join health clubs or become marathon runners. But it <u>is</u> important to get the blood flowing to the brain by whatever means you can handle. Maybe the easiest and least expensive is just taking a daily brisk walk. You set the pace, the time of day and route.

Dori can't always get out to walk, especially

with snow on the ground. But she determined, nonetheless, to continue her exercises even if it had to be indoors. She sets a certain length of time to walk all over the house, covering every room. By the time the buzzer goes off to indicate her time is up, the feeling in her legs says she's done herself a big favor!

Stay-at-home exercise is often the most comfortable and convenient route to go. Seriously consider investing in some of the exercise equipment now available for home use:

- an exercise bike
- stairclimber
- cross country ski machine

or

- rowing machine.

**REMINDER** Save yourself some really sore muscles by starting out easy on whatever exercise plan you might attempt. Treat your body with kindness . . . with your heart and emotions already torn apart, your muscles don't care to follow suit!

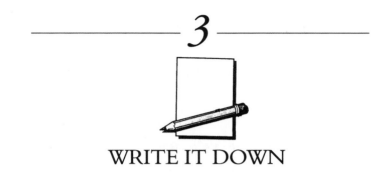

WRITE IT DOWN

It seems crazy to even <u>consider</u> mentioning the benefits of keeping a journal about your feelings and what you're thinking from day to day. After all, in the midst of the worst experience of your life. . . when you are lucky to remember your own <u>name</u>, how in the world are you supposed to put your fragmented thoughts on paper?

Believe me . . . keeping some kind of journal hadn't been something I thought would be of any specific benefit to me either! Yet, when I kind of "fell" into the idea right after Greg's death, I began to realize (as I moved further down the road) just what a godsend it was!

It started quite simply: I had a piece of paper by the phone and as special things kept happening or friends did something exceptional that touched the depths of my raw emotions, I wanted to be sure not to forget them. So, I'd write down a phrase or two that served as my reminder. Some were:

- Sandra's roast dinner first night
- Nanny & Bruce: yard wk. before funeral;
- Gas station attendant's help;
- Kathy – pie;
- 2 cords of wood delivered;
- 25' phone cord appeared!
- Car help for winter

After awhile, I added notations about some accomplishments for different days:

- Paid all bills
- Made it through first work day
- Handled unexpected five – hr. airport delay alone

The average person, untouched by grief, wouldn't think of these last three things as any big deal. BUT . . . on a scale of 1 – 10 (with 10 being highest degree of difficulty), any <u>one</u> of these is a 12 (that's not a misprint!) to new survivors.

In the course of jotting down a few lines here and there, my sheet of paper was filled. In order to continue my "musings", I had to buy a little notebook.

But, you might think, "Well, where is the big advantage in all of this for me?" As the weeks and months dragged by and I might be facing a particularly bad day or a situation to dread, I'd look back over my list of past accomplishments, thinking, "Wow, Carlene, remember when THAT was such a big deal and now it's behind you! You've come this far so I don't think what you're agonizing over now can loom much larger than that!" It showed me clearly where I'd been, what I'd felt and how I might be improving (ever so slightly). I started to see that this journal-keeping was one of the best thing I'd ever done!

Your reaction to this idea may be similar to Carrie's. I related how much this had helped me in the past, as I recommended it to her, a new survivor. She admitted later:

> *"I went home and thought: I'll be jiggered if I'm going to start keeping some dumb diary like a silly teenager – forget it! But a few months later, I started writing down a few things that I had been doing. Now as I look back on it, I think, 'Why in the world didn't you write down stuff in the beginning like Carlene suggested?' It would have been a huge boost to my fragile self-image, reading what I'd felt at the beginning*

*and how far I had progressed from
there !"*

Maybe you are sitting there saying to yourself, "That is all well and good for someone brand-new in grief. But I am a year or two beyond that and so it's just too late for me to start this journal-keeping now. Right?" Wrong!

You still find yourself swamped with unexpected waves of grief, don't you? Hopefully, it's not quite the asphyxiating feeling you had at the start, but it's still very real and all-together crushing just the same. And . . . aren't there things you are still accomplishing every day or week? How about having to sell your son's old but beloved car or summoning the courage to attend that first baby shower after your baby's death? Have you managed to go to another funeral or get in touch with someone else who has suffered a loss similar to yours? Any of these are terrific signs showing you're making progress. But unless you write them down, they'll soon fade from memory. Without seeing, in print, just what were major things at one time, you won't be able to fully gauge your growth through grief.

Ok, maybe it isn't that bad of an idea . . . maybe it does have some merits. But, you say, can't you remember how difficult it was at this time to even pick up a pen? "There's no way on God's green earth," you continue, "I'm going to be able to write down even four words in a row that make any sense whatsoever!"

That's an excellent point. How about trying what worked for Erlene? Hearing of my journal-keeping idea, she realized writing very much wasn't feasible. However, she noticed the good-size calendar on her wall had large blank squares for each day of the month. She determined this would be her journal and so began writing a phrase or two in the square for each day. Sometimes, it was only a few times during the week. She reported this method worked perfectly and it was easy to look back over the last month (or six months or more) and notice some milestones.

Go ahead . . . give it a try! I honestly realize it may be the hardest thing I will suggest you do in this entire book and yet . . . its value to you in the months ahead can't be measured. You're worth the effort!

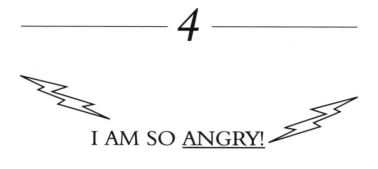

4

I AM SO <u>ANGRY!</u>

One of the most important people to you in the world is gone. It doesn't seem fair ... it isn't right! If there were any justice this surely wouldn't have happened. With all the terrorists, dictators, criminals, bums and jerks in the world, why is this happening to me?

There may be many things or people or circumstances where your anger is directed:

- the drunk driver
- the doctor/surgeon
- hospitals/incompetent staff
- weather/road conditions
- our criminal system
- school
- the car manufacturer
- God

In the logical, rational mind of the person untouched by grief, anything on this list (and a million others besides!) can be explained away, perhaps semi-justified and <u>maybe</u> even accepted. BUT . . . to survivors, someone more precious than life itself is gone and somebody or something has got to be at fault.

It's easy to listen to a doctor's clinical counsel that explains what anger can do to the human body and how it can so consume someone, their health is never the same.But what is not easy is to just accept those words on faith alone and simply stop being angry! Lectures don't cause anger to disappear.

I don't know all the answers but let me share a few ideas I've discovered about working on anger. Maybe one or more of them might help you.

Knowing you're not alone in being angry is very important. Maybe your anger is directed at the person who is gone and then you think this has to be really insane! Well, no, it's not! That is one of the most common ways to react. Wives are trying to handle the kids, juggle the finances and keep up the house and thus are furious at husbands who would leave them in this mess. The same holds true for husbands left behind.

Parents who lose a teenager or adult child may also become deeply resentful seeing the natural order of the universe being out of "whack" since <u>children</u>

are supposed to eventually bury their <u>parents</u>, instead of vice versa. The child may have been walking on the now-thawing pond when he'd been told not to, or could have been climbing over a fence that said No Trespassing when he came in contact with high-voltage wires. The parent is doubly angry, not only at fate, but also at the child for taking a chance on disobeying and ending up paying with his life.

On the deepest level of anger in grief are those who are forced to deal with the circumstances surrounding a suicide. The guilt associated with constant "why's" and "if only's" are all-consuming to every survivor . . . family or friend a-like.

What can help? Barbie said she began to find recovery from her husband's motorcycle accident when she would shout at his picture. Putting into words how infuriated she was at being left, lessened her anger considerably. Telling our special person how angry we are is not a one-time episode. It must be repeated whenever those indignant feelings are boiling near the surface.

Someone else said they felt a little uneasy trying to scream at a picture of their loved one. Instead, they wrote page after page, expressing their intense feelings. Being able to put their thoughts down in black-and-white helped prevent keeping all that anger stored internally and later developing physical problems.

Annie lost her young husband to suicide and was left with a little baby. She has mentioned that even though it has been over three years now, she still finds herself so angry at him for leaving, her emotions are sometimes hard to contain. Wisely, she's been seeing a counselor once a month for an extended period of time. (That's another thing about grief: it is NEVER wrong to go seek professional help! Only the truly courageous are willing to do so.) This counselor suggested the following exercise for releasing pent-up anger:

Get a tennis racket . . . even an old one with broken strings, like you might uncover in a Goodwill store. Put all the pillows found in the house in a pile in the middle of a room. Kneel down by the pile and raise the racket (using both hands) high over your head, arms fully extended. Bring down the racket on the pillows with as much force as you can. The energy of being angry will flow from you, to the racket and out. Do this over and over and over again. It can't hurt the racket too much, you can't destroy the furniture if the pillows are on the floor and you aren't too likely to self-destruct by trying this either! That was a new idea to me and it sounds like a winner!

So what could you try when you're angry with God? Someone once said that God is big enough to handle your anger . . . He can face any confrontation you want to have with Him. I believe that.

Feel free to tell Him you're angry, don't understand what has happened and you especially don't know "why." If you are comfortable writing things down, write letters to God. Tell Him exactly how you feel and what you think of Him. This may take many, many pages, written over a long period of time. By seeing your anger expressed in print instead of that emotion being a series of unspoken, tormenting thoughts, it becomes easier to acknowledge how you feel, cope with it and begin to release it.

Why not go to a park, or row out in the middle of a lake, walk back into the woods or out in a field . . . and yell at God. Scream at Him, telling Him how you're feeling. Wow! So much tension will be released because you're physically expressing your internal emotions. It's healthy!

The idea for helping us overcome much of our anger appears here to be doing something <u>physical</u> . . . writing, yelling, swinging a racket, talking. Someone I know observed that taking a hatchet to a back-yard tree was an astounding balm to ease the raging soul. (Now, if you live in the desert or on the plains of the Midwest, this "George Washington" attack may be a little more difficult to imitate!!)

Others have mentioned that just punching the daylights out of an old stuffed animal (please . . . not the kid's favorite!) or attacking the garbage can with a baseball bat really helped release a lot of pressure.

 How many times have you heard this now . . . it's normal . . . even anger! Choosing to release it through expression is the rough part. It takes work . . . but then anything worthwhile usually does!

5

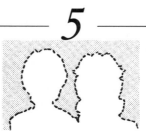

YOU TALK TO PICTURES TOO?

Do you ever go around the house talking to yourself . . . even talking to a picture of the one who is gone? If so . . . welcome to the club!

Greg sometimes would ask me what I would miss most about him if he died. I'd say things like "Oh, your smile" or "your laugh." But it wasn't until he was really gone (and all of you know exactly what I mean!) that the most obvious thing I missed was his physical presence: being there to share with, discuss the day's events, what had happened in our families or who I had met. I just couldn't believe how incredible it was to miss that mutual sharing together. Whew!

Toni came up with a clever way to share with her husband. She sat down and tape recorded the things she was feeling, what she wanted to share, what she was missing. Then, playing back the tapes, she took her place as the listener. It was easier to formulate ideas, she said, by <u>hearing</u> how they sounded, rather than just <u>thinking</u> them.

I was never wise enough to think of doing that, but I do know what relief and comfort I received from talking to Greg's picture as it hung on my wall. I'd come home from work and say (right out-loud),

"You won't <u>believe</u> who
I met today!"
Or "Listen to what so-and-so did!"

It felt so good, getting to share with him, even though in my more sane moments (which were few and far between!) I knew he wasn't really listening. It was still soothing . . . getting to express my thoughts.

Donna shared a funny illustration about this. She and her husband were good friends with Clyde and his wife. Clyde's wife passed away after a long illness. Many months later, a mutual friend of both couples confided to Donna:

"Did you hear about poor Clyde? I
hear he's so far gone with this grief

business, he's even talking to his
wife's picture!"

Donna was equally dismayed to hear that and said so. A few months later, however, Donna's husband also passed away. It wasn't but a few weeks later she caught herself talking to <u>her</u> husband's picture on the piano. She wryly concluded,

"All of a sudden this previous
conversation about
Clyde came back to me and I started
to chuckle to myself . . . Clyde
wasn't so
crazy after all!"

 Don't feel you're a candidate for the "funny farm" if you're comfortable talking to a dead person's picture! You're most certainly normal and the only ones who might raise an eyebrow over your actions are those who have not been where you are now.

6

HANG ON TO IT
OR THROW IT OUT?

This is really a complicated issue, sometimes, isn't it? It doesn't matter what time frame you use . . . a week after the funeral, six months or a couple of years. At some point you are forced to sit down and decide just what to keep for awhile, what to throw out or give away and what will always be saved as a treasured memory. It seems like each of us does some of all three but not all at the same time and not all in the same proportion to someone else.

Do you leave your daughter's room just the way it is now? What about your husband's home office? How do you decide whether to sell or keep your son's cherished mountain bike; your Mom's knick-knacks; the baby's christening outfit or that favorite blanket? The list is endless and this dilemma isn't always just being forced to deal with household items, either.

One doctor's wife observed,

*"I was doing pretty good when I
sold his office, but as I watched his
so-familiar desk being carried out, it
about broke my heart. That desk was
<u>part</u> of him."*

I remember thinking I'd better hurriedly get rid
of Greg's things around the house and garage while
I was still slightly sane (!) because I feared an insan-
ity attack was awaiting me around each corner.

What made it much easier for me (and probably
for you, too) was the joy in sharing his special
"treasures" with others in our circle of family and
friends. I believed they would treat these things
with the same love and care Greg had been giving
them over the years. Sending a lot of things to the
Goodwill may be a way to help quickly empty out a
bedroom, the whole house or the garage. But it's a
sensible thought to check first with family and
friends.

A family with three teenage boys lost their Dad
suddenly. Claudia didn't have any desire to go
through all of his belongings right away. But a couple
of years later, forced to move, she checked with the

boys to see if they were interested in each keeping some of Dad's jewelry (rings, cufflinks, tie clasp, etc.) They expressed no interest and so she sold some of it and gave other items away to friends. Now, fifteen years later, the boys have commented how much they wish some of these special momentos of Dad were still around. How was she to know they would change their minds?

This is a good illustration to consider when deciding what to do with items such as that. If it's possible to store some, put away jewelry and pictures (maybe in a safe deposit box) and as the years go by, if the kids decide they'd like to have something of Mom or Dad's, you'll have it available for them.

Another mother gives us a good example of the advantages of keeping some things around the house for awhile. With Christmas approaching, she had zero enthusiasm for shopping (no kidding!) Wandering into her husband's home library, she decided to look through the shelves of books, searching for one that was best suited to each child's specific interests. Sitting down at his desk, she then took the time to write on the inside front cover of each book, the traits about that child Mom and Dad thought were especially unique and notable. These books were wrapped as the children's Christmas gifts. Can you imagine what a treasure that book would become as the kids grew up? At any time they could open the book jacket to read its now-familiar script and think, "Wow! That's what Dad thought about me!" [1]

So , after reading these examples you ask: Is there a set guideline for deciding what to keep and for how long? There's no real answer to this and that's important to understand. Every person's internal "clock", used to judge when the "right" time comes, runs at a different speed. Relatives or well-meaning friends may want to suggest when the time seems appropriate to <u>them</u> but once again . . . it is only the survivor who can make the final decision on this.

Loni wrote that she wasn't given the option about what to do with her husband's things. At the house following his funeral, her in-laws went through the rooms, taking what they assumed should be theirs of his! She was in no condition that day to even notice what was happening. This makes me shudder and also reminds me to again be grateful to my own in-laws for going out of their way to let me know everything was mine to keep or dispose of in whatever time line made me most comfortable.

I asked Charlotte if she had saved any special things of her son's, as time passed, after his death.

> *"Even though Tim's been gone ten years, in the bottom of my dresser drawer at home, I still have his small rug folded up, that used to be in front of his bed. In that drawer I also have a used pop can he'd left in his room the day he died. People would think I was nuts, "she continued, "so I don't go around broadcasting this. But sometimes I just look in that drawer and feel good that I have something he touched and used."*

Doug and Ginny have taken some years to tackle the job of going through Drew's apartment possessions. During this time they didn't decide to turn a room in their home into an untouchable "shrine" for Drew, but just left boxes stored under their basement stairs, waiting until they felt like handling it together.

Many parents and spouses have kept a special box in which to put many of the momentos to save:

- their child's favorite toys
- hair strands in a hairbrush
- wedding/photo albums
- birth/death certificates
- sympathy cards

(In "Will Anything Make One Day Better Than Another" there is a terrific suggestion that enlarges the idea of a treasured box . . .) For now, I feel good about having my "Greg Box" downstairs where I can take a private moment now and then, to look at, read and remember the past.

I'm always learning there are new definitions of possessions you end up addressing. Let me share one with you.

I listened to a fascinating conversation in my support group one night that started with a quiet confession:

One gal mentioned that although it had been a couple of years since her husband's death, she still hadn't been able to bring herself to throw away all his pills sitting on her cupboard shelf. She said looking at them was like reading a diary of how he slowly slipped away, judging by the dates

and increased dosages on the bottles.
A look of wonder came over another
gal's face as she suddenly interrupted,
"Oh, do <u>you</u> keep those too? I keep
worrying someone will look in my
cupboard, discover those old pill
bottles still there and conclude I'm
completely nuts for not having
thrown them away a long time ago.
What a relief to hear somebody <u>else</u>
does that too!"

It is a terrific feeling to know that other, very sane, normal survivors do things like you do, isn't it?

You need to remind yourself that every survivor's time for dealing with possessions is normal. Whatever you feel most comfortable with . . . do it!

7

OOPS!

I CAN'T SHUT OFF
"THE WATER WORKS!"

Those tears . . . they flow constantly . . . and come without warning, making us feel so vulnerable. I remember getting some flowers after Greg's funeral. On the card was written the paraphrase of a Scripture verse:

> *"He bottles our every tear,*
> *He remembers our every sigh."*

My sister was looking over my shoulder when I opened the card and I heard her mutter to herself, "Well, He's sure got a bucketload of mine!" Most of you probably agree . . . you could start a flood if your every tear had first been stored and then suddenly released!

Recently, I read of an innovative way to accelerate past some of that initial teary period everyone finds so hard to endure.

In her book <u>So Stick A Geranium</u> <u>In Your Hat And Be Happy</u>,[1] Barbara Johnson shares the following experience:

Barbara had just lost her second son in less than five years. Going through a store checkout line, she noticed a clerk dissolved in tears. Speaking to her, Barbara learned the lady had also recently lost a child. She was finding it increasingly more difficult for her to work and try to turn off the tears that were flowing nonstop. Barbara offered her own method for coping with those "buckets" of tears. Here it is:

> *Go find the saddest tape or record you can find ... maybe one from long ago that brings back lots of painful memories. Plan a time of the day when everyone is out of the house. Unplug the phone, go in the bedroom and set a timer for 30 minutes. Then sob your heart out for the entire 30 minutes. Pound the pillow if you feel like it. The next day, do the same thing, but set the timer for only 29 minutes. The next day, make it 28 minutes, etc. Do this*

for 30 days and it will help you
dump a great load of that pent-up
grief.

The clerk tried this idea and phoned Barbara to let her know that even in just the span of a week's worth of crying, she was already feeling better and able to turn off most of the tears while at work. That, in itself, is an accomplishment!

Of course, you are sensible enough to understand that grief is far too extensive to be "cured" by one month of tears but Barbara's tip is designed to just help take that edge off the emotional volcano bubbling inside.

Men often feel pressured from society that being "masculine" involves holding back those tears and never letting the hurt show. It's far healthier to do as Joel did. He said,

"I was so overcome by this loss, I
didn't have the energy to pretend it
didn't hurt. When I felt the tears
coming, I just went ahead and
reached for my hankie and let the
tears come – in front of friends or
with family. By swallowing my pride

*and letting them see my grief, I think
it helped others to understand and
kept me from exploding inside."*

Children often have a different schedule for
tears than adults. And each child will grieve in his
own way. Caroline shared an interesting example:

Three days after her son Todd's death, Caroline's sixteen year old boy ran into the house, hyper-
ventilating. He sobbingly confessed he hadn't
thought about Todd for a few hours. He kept saying
he was so bad to have not been thinking of him
every single minute. Wisely, Caroline quickly reas-
sured him it was ok to go do something with friends
and get his mind off all that was going on. Taking a
break from dwelling on the tragedy did not show
any less expression of love for Todd.

It's tough to be thinking of how the kids are
reacting to a death in the family, while the adults are
attempting to cope with the news themselves. Did
you know there is a wonderful new sixteen-minute
video now out called "A Child's View of Grief?" It is
a series of clear, informative interviews on grief
with kids of various ages. For a nominal fee you can
send for a copy – from:

Hazen & Jaeger Funeral Homes
1306 N. Monroe
Spokane, WA 99205
Attn: Dwayne Harmon

I highly recommend it!

Crying . . . tears . . . sobbing . . . sniffling . . . all are normal in grief. Sadly, it seems that some survivors are trying to earn an Oscar for *"Best Tearless Performance While Under Pressure."* The only thing you end up winning this way is an ulcer, often soon followed by an emotional breakdown.

Give yourself the freedom to cry.

GREAT IDEAS

MAGAZINES WRITTEN JUST FOR SURVIVORS

Were you aware there are some great publications written just for people like you who are struggling to get through one twenty-four period at a time? I can highly recommend both of the following:

The first one is **Bereavement**, published six times a year. It addresses all types of grief, from miscarriage, to infant loss; the loss of adult children, parents, brothers, sisters and spouses. It is written by those who have experienced grief and want to share their feelings as well as a few features by regular columnists. The editor, Andrea Gambill, lost her beloved daughter in the mid-'70's and started this magazine because she saw such a need among survivors. Her first-hand knowledge of grief is evident in the articles, poems and writings chosen for print. A year's subscription is $29.00 and can be addressed to:

Bereavement Publishing, Inc.
8133 Telegraph Drive
Colorado Springs, CO 80920

What first caught my eye about this publication was a comment on its informational brochure. It says:

> *"Thanks for your interest . . . and, hopefully, thanks for the opportunity to be in touch. We'll keep visiting until you don't need us any more . . . and, from the heart, we can say, 'We'll share your satisfaction the day you decide **not** to renew your subscription.'"*

Wow! Does that mean recovery from grief just <u>might</u> be possible? There <u>is</u> light at the end of this long, dark tunnel? What a positive promise!

THEOS is the other fine magazine. For the cost of $26.00, a set of eight different issues will be sent to you. THEOS is written by widows and widowers for others who have also lost a spouse. It's so easy to relate to what they say because their writings describe how all survivors feel.

The eight issues are:

- *Grief Steps I and II*
- *Grief Sounds I and II*
- *Days & Seasons of Grief*
- *Death: A Family Affair*
- *Grief and Sympathy*
  and
- *Singles, Pairs & Social Circles*

You can send your subscription check to:
THEOS

322 Blvd. of the Allies #105
Pittsburgh, PA 15222
1-412-471-7779

Kitty, one of my support group members, said her kids come home and say, "Mom, why are you <u>still</u> sitting in that chair? You stay there all the time." She explained, "What I'm doing is sitting here reading my THEOS magazines over and over again. They are about the only thing making much sense to me right now!"

Marriana added that she read the first issue and then put it away, only to discover it again two weeks later. As she glanced through it the second time, she discovered all new things she hadn't remembered reading before.

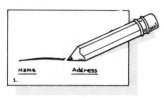

Make it a top priority item in your budget to subscribe to one of these publications. Each of you now belongs (certainly not by choice!) to that unique club . . . "For Survivors Only." So even when you find it impossible for others to know how you feel and when you realize you can't concentrate on anything else in print, turn to the magazines that enable you to instantly relate to the authors because they also share your pain.

Treat yourself!

9

MAKE PLANS NOW!

HELP! THAT FIRST YEAR DATE IS COMING UP!

What **can** you do when that day is approaching? It seems like such a day to dread. After all, you barely survived it the first time and even now, your mind is going over the details of the weeks leading up to the fateful day. Sometimes, doesn't it seem like <u>forever</u> since you talked to, saw and touched your special person? Yet, other times, it seems just like <u>yesterday</u>? This, then, appears to be a day you attempt to escape . . . or try to ignore (impossible!) . . . or just go nuts or something! Instead of any of these, look at some tips I've listed here, find some that might appeal to you, and make plans well in advance for that day.

When I was anticipating my first death anniversary, I was talking to a gal who had lived through hers many years before. As I told her of my fears, she said:

"Oh, I didn't think like that at all!
*I was **anxious** for the day to come*
and was relieved when it arrived!"

Well, I privately assumed she was definitely some kind of "whacko" (!) but then she went on to explain:

"I felt like it was a wonderful
***accomplishment** to have made it*
through that awful first year,
enduring the horrible holidays, our
anniversary, his birthday, etc. I
looked at it as a major achievement to
have come this far alone, instead of
something awful to run away from."

Hum m m . . . it took me awhile to ponder what she'd shared but now I believe it **is** true and she **was** right. It **is** a bit easier of a day, if along with the natural torrent of memories that flood your mind, is the thought that this is a day to be proud of yourself for having made it this far. After all, 365 days ago you were positive you couldn't make it through the next day or the next week let alone, 12 long months. But you HAVE made it, haven't you?? Commend yourself . . . brag on you a little . . . you deserve it!

An especially precious thought comes from Bill Ermatinger, who lost his daughter, Kathy. He explains that there are special days for important people in our nation, such as George Washington, Abraham Lincoln and Martin Luther King. We recognize these and set aside specific days to honor their lives and memories. Awhile after Kathy's death, he decided to set aside a special day to honor her life and memory, choosing the anniversary of her death as that day. Over the years it became a unique tradition for him. If it was a work day, he would take it off, going first to the cemetery in the morning. There he'd visit her grave and share with her the year's happenings and what he'd been doing. Then, the rest of the day, he'd do something special . . . go to the seashore, walk along the beach or wander through a museum or art gallery. Sometimes he chose to try a day trip.

He concludes:

> *"I don't expect the world to join in this celebration, but neither will I let the year be complete without this special day being included in the calendar of hearts."* [1]

When I read that, I thought – why can't every-one have a "Kathy's Holiday" – a day set aside to honor the memory of the one who is gone. My thanks to Bill for that heartwarming approach to a difficult day!

Try writing a letter to your special person . . . including some of the accomplishments you've made this year, while missing them so much . . . even making mention of mistakes you've made and what you miss about them being away. Take it to the cemetery, leaving it on the gravestone.

If this anniversary date falls on a Sunday, donate the altar flowers for your church and have the bulletin make mention of the occasion and in whose memory they were given.

Addy's husband's grave was hundreds of miles away from where she presently lives. Being unable to return there for his death date, she tried something new last year. She asked some of us in our support group where our husband's graves were located around here and then on Monty's day, she went to our graves, putting flowers there, in her husband's honor. Neat idea! (By the way, I wanted to run out to the cemetery ahead of her and exclaim, "Honey, somebody's coming to visit you . . . isn't that super??")

It is important, I think, to realize most of your friends will **NOT** be acknowledging this date (or a birthday or wedding anniversary, either.) Many of them think if they don't bring this date up (by sending a card or flowers or just in conversation), you won't remember it. I often think, "WHAT?! Forget a birthday we celebrated for years? Not recall the day that changed my life forever? Who are you kidding??!" Someone else added: "I simply refuse to believe that nobody else remembers these days but me!"

However, if close friends or relatives <u>do</u> remember it, then it's important to brag on them for it, with thanks, showing your appreciation.

Don't Overlook

Why? Well, they probably did this with "fear and trembling", wondering if it was a big mistake. Your prompt reassurance to them that what they did was a great comfort, will make them bolder to try this same thing some <u>other</u> day, some <u>other</u> time, with some <u>other</u> survivor who is also craving just that same kind of support and remembrance they gave to you.

10

Coming Up!

WHAT ABOUT THOSE "OTHER" HOLIDAYS?

Birthdays are certainly rugged times to survive, aren't they? Mom doesn't have a birthday party to plan any more or a cake to bake and decorate. You walk into a department store and it dawns on you that now there's no reason to go shopping in the baby section or the men's area. You notice people looking through the display for birthday cards and you force yourself to move on before you run up to the customers exclaiming, "Do you know how **lucky** you are to get to buy that birthday card?!"

Often it feels good just to take flowers to the cemetery on this day. Other survivors have made it a point to give a donation to their favorite charity on this birthdate in their loved one's name.

Andrea died at nineteen in a flash flood last summer. Her parents are naturally having a real struggle dealing with this unexpected loss. But facing her upcoming birthday, they decided to try something different. Dressing up in their best clothes, they treated themselves to a dinner at the nicest restaurant in their area. They wanted it to be a time to <u>honor</u> Andrea, even as they were mourning her loss. I liked that way of looking at it!

Erica proves what was stated in an earlier part of this book: If it feels good, go ahead and do it and don't worry about what others think! Her husband's birthday was approaching and she was missing the opportunity to make him a cake, buy a present or even find a special card. So she bought two cupcakes at the bakery, put a candle in each and she and her sister sang "Happy Birthday" to her hubby! She commented,

> *"People would think I was balmy if they'd looked in the window but I didn't care. It just felt so good to remember him like that!"*

Some families have decided on planting a tree or shrub for each birthday that passes – not just in their own yard, but in another family member's yard, the school or at their church. One Mom said it felt good to look out her window in the spring and see Dale's tree in bloom.

My Mom and I felt good taking out a big "Happy Birthday" balloon to leave at Dad's grave. We couldn't give him a party but it made us feel better to acknowledge that day in a visual way!

Other days that aren't easy (come to think of it, are there any that <u>are</u> easy?!?) are Mother's and Father's Days. Those who have lost a child or parent cannot bear to see the commercials coming on, advertising these days well in advance. These suggestions that broadcast how best to remember Mom or Dad this year give rise to another shooting pain of grief.

Dwaine shared that every father-son commercial (whether fishing, fixing cars, etc.) which insinuates that special relationship, is devasting to him. He said it's just <u>another</u> reminder that he doesn't have his son's companionship to appreciate any more.

Just as you must give yourself the needed permission to cry, so you must also permit yourself to skip events guaranteed to "finish you off" (emotionally) for the day. Events like attending church on Mother's or Father's Day, need to be thought through carefully. If roses are being handed out in an assembly to mothers and you just lost your baby

. . . this first or second year might be good times to avoid attending. One mother I know finds Mother's Day always difficult so she annually is away from church on that day. Why put herself through an obvious emotional wringer?

Tami remembers:

"When our church started handing
out flowers to the mothers, I had to
run out of the service and downstairs,
where I could sob my heart out.
Little Josh was gone and now his
Dad is too and there <u>*was*</u> *no joy for*
me in Mother's Day."

Valentine's Day is another "winner" in the holiday schedule, isn't it? There is nothing that can take the place of a spouse's love and recognition on that day. Lori's daughter pleasantly surprised her Mom on this first holiday alone. She went through all the Valentine cards Dad had given Mom through the many, many years and had them sitting up, individually, on the dining room table, when Lori got home. It was hard but also special to look through each one and remember again how much love she had shared in the past.

Although it is not always included with the regular lists of "holidays" Halloween is a pretty stressful day for bereaved parents of small children. Should they leave home before the arrival all the little happy faces at their door? Or should they try to dress up the rest of their kids and take them out as is the tradition? It might be wise to ask someone else, such as close neighbors or a relative, to handle the trick-or-treating this year. Seems like there's always <u>another</u> "holiday hurdle" lurking around the corner . . . right?

An individual kind of holiday is a 25th or 50th wedding anniversary. What a time for the loneliness of "what might have been!" But I recently met an older lady who made the best of this wistful time in her life. She said,

> *"I decided even if my hubby wasn't*
> *here, I wanted to remember and*
> *recognize our special day anyway. So*
> *on our 50th anniversary, I bought*
> *myself the prettiest sweater I could*
> *find. I wear it often now and*
> *remember it as my '50th' sweater!*
> *I told this to some of my friends*
> *(their 50th dates are coming up soon)*

and they, too, agreed it was a good
idea and plan to go buy themselves
something special in honor of their
day!"

What a sweet thought!

These holidays, like all others, have to be planned in advance. To just suddenly have the big day come with no "game plan" of how to keep busy (whether to attend something or not; how to handle the kids and yourself) doesn't work. Idle time on your hands gives way quickly to more loneliness and stress.

Be kind to yourself . . .you've earned it!

11

COUNTDOWN for

CHRISTMAS
(Bah-humbug!)

All of us would agree, I believe, that when thinking of holidays to avoid, Christmas ranks right at the top! It's impossible to dread, alarming to anticipate and gut-wrenching to endure. In fact . . . if you're reading this book right now and you **have** survived a first Christmas . . . raise your hand. (Oh, go ahead – who's going to notice – or care?) As long as your hand is up for a second, turn the palm of your hand around, reach over and give yourself a pat on the back. Really! Go for it! Goodness knows, you deserve to be commended. Of course it wasn't easy but then, nothing seems to be a "piece of cake" in grief, does it?

Slowly I've been learning a few things that you could try to make next year's holiday a little more survivable. You can try any, or all, or none of these ideas – whatever sounds good.

One survivor said she bought the prettiest Christmas candle she could find. Then every night through December, she lit it for the whole time she was home. It was like a special, warming presence in her home and a unique way to remember her special person being gone. I've suggested this to many people and they've told me later it really <u>was</u> a good idea!

I believe it's also important to pamper your-selves as survivors, during this time of the year. Go out and find something you'd really like (or maybe it's something you need) and then buy that gift for you for Christmas. You can even wrap it up, put it under the tree (that is, if you've been braver than ME and have one set up!) and then open it when-ever you feel like it. You might take the unwrapped gift to a friend and ask them to wrap it for you, so you'll be surprised at the shiny paper and pretty bows they use. Try taking your unwrapped present to one of the big department stores that do gift wrap and from their many designs, pick out one that is your favorite. Let them do a great job on your "gift to you."

I spotted a peach ski jacket I really liked, my first Christmas. Having admired it for awhile, but think-ing it was too extravagant for my budget, I put off its purchase. Then Christmas Eve arrived and I had to work that day, as a clerk, waiting on merry last-minute shoppers in the store. While they were disgustingly happy and busy wishing me "Merry Christmas," my chest got tighter and heavier as I tried to stifle my emotions. It was debatable if I could hold on long enough to drive home before bawling my head off. So I thought: why not buy that jacket. Maybe you <u>do</u> deserve a treat today! I'm so glad I did! It **did** make me feel better and even now, although I don't wear it much any more, it hangs in my closet as a silent reminder to me that I **did** survive that first tough Christmas.

Some folks say that fixing the turkey and getting the dinner out is the toughest part of the holiday because they should be fixing this food for the one who is gone . . . and they can't. I think you need to (again) give yourself permission to change the traditions of Christmas, if you wish. If the idea of turkey is depressing, decide on a new menu. Switch to ham or maybe prime rib.

If you always opened presents in the morning, do them on Christmas Eve instead. (At least make the suggestion and see what your family thinks.) If you always hosted dinner at your home, ask someone else to do it. Plan to do your shopping early in the morning, before all the shops are filled with the merriest people and clerks you'll ever see! Or . . . vow you'll do your shopping by mail catalogue or at least before the middle of October when the stores and malls are fully decorated.

If you can't shop and yet you <u>must</u> give presents, why not make out checks (big or small) to cover those on your list? Everyone can use money; it's always the right "size" and "color" and the stress you've saved yourself by skipping shopping, will be well worth it!

Maybe sitting down to eat a lovely dinner with a beautifully decorated table setting is a bit too much to ask. Some say they've tried doing it and end up in the bedroom in tears. Well, why not serve the meal on TV trays. You could use the table for a buffet set-up and nobody would have reason to question it.

Another idea you might try . . . if your family each has their own Christmas sock. Suddenly there's an empty one . . . it's hard to decide whether to hang it up, put it back in storage or just <u>what</u> to do. One family decided to hang up their child's stocking and then each family member wrote a sentence (or two or three) on a notecard . . . to the one who was no longer there. They could tell something about what had happened over the last year, maybe something they missed or even a funny occurrence. Then the notes were put in the stocking and the family could choose to either read them out loud together or any one could get the notes out and read them alone, at any time. These could be saved from year to year, making it a nice tradition to look back and see what has been happening to the family in the intervening years. We tried that this year as my Dad died in the fall. I really had a good time writing down things to share with him. A P.S. on my card added,

"You'll be delighted to know, Dad that the Reds swept the A's in the World Series, four games straight! I just knew you'd love hearing that!"

Allie was feeling sad that when her husband died, she was left with a baby daughter who is now growing up never knowing her Dad. So this Christmas (her third without Martin) she sent out her traditional Christmas letter with a "twist." Near the end of it, she mentioned that Marcy was starting to inquire about Daddy and as her Mom, Allie wished to give her a better idea of who Dad really was. So she requested people write back things they might have done with Martin, funny things they laughed about, things they noticed as he was growing up, or characteristics special to him, etc.

She further added she was making up a scrapbook for Marcy and would include all of their notes in it. Later Marcy could sit down and read through this book about Dad . . . even later "introducing" Dad to her friends. Obviously, the great side benefit was that Allie would get to read these letters herself and learn new things about Martin she might not have known before. People did respond to this plea and even a couple of men wrote back two and three page letters containing their memories. Terrific! No matter what age of the person you are missing, this would be a good way to add to the "Memory Book" we'll discuss in the next section.

Did you know there are flat, brass Christmas ornaments available in engraving shops, that can display a photo of our special person? I discovered that last year and have been buying quite a few to send to friends, family and fellow survivors. The oval picture opening in the center of a bell or tree shape, has a little plastic cover so the picture won't get scratched. You can also have your special person's name engraved on the ornament. I enjoyed giving one to my sister (engraved "Dad") and one to my niece (with "Grandpa" on it). Mom hung hers on the little artificial tree she had and said she enjoyed getting up every day and saying "hi" to Dad on the tree! I cut out a snapshot of Greg and put it in an ornament, sending it to his Mom. Later I asked how it looked on her tree and she laughed,

"Oh, I was so excited to get it, I haven't had time to hang it up yet! I keep it in my purse to show everybody 'uptown' when I see them on the street. I'll get it to the tree eventually!!" (Obviously, she's residing in a small community!)

I don't sell these ornaments or get a commission on them (!) but just hoped that if you were made aware of their existence, you could search the stores through 'til you found some. If you are really interested yet cannot locate them anywhere in your area, please feel free to write me. I'll put you in touch with my local distributor.

This turned out to be the holiday with the longest list of helps but when it also happens to be the biggest and toughest holiday to confront through the year . . . you, the new survivor, are entitled to all the advice available.

12

WILL ANYTHING MAKE ONE DAY ANY BETTER THAN ANOTHER?

The instant cure for grief has yet to be invented (although most of us would surely volunteer to be a guinea pig for any new method suggested!) However, here are some ways others have used to help them feel a little better in day-to-day living. Let me share these with you.

One fellow enjoyed having friends come to see old movies (or slides) of past vacations with his wife. It was special to get to see them himself (after so many years) but the privilege of getting to share Lillian with others was unbeatable! Maybe you've taken family vacations with others and you're thinking reviewing all the pictures would be too emotionally draining. You could try it as an experiment, including only very close friends. See if it doesn't make you glad/sad all at the same time. Usually the accent is more on the "glad," though.

Emily has tried this same thing, only just enjoys

getting out the old slide projector (she confides it's from another era!) and sitting down to watch slides all alone on long winter evenings. Many a night is taken up with this project. The preciousness of the memories this brings, she says, far exceeds the sad realization that Harry isn't sitting there next to her to enjoy the show too.

After their son's accidental drowning, Tom and Estelle dreaded going back to work. Tom was especially leery because his job was on the college campus. How could he stand to be around kids Mike's age? He now says going back was the best thing he ever did! He was astonished to discover that seeing other kids, talking with them and being involved in their lives, made him feel closer to Mike. Both he and Estelle agreed that getting out of the house and back on the job, surrounded eight hours a day with other people and circumstances, made recovery a bit easier.

Bonnie took up volunteer work . . . not that long after her husband's death. It forced her out of the house (and "force" it is; staying home "cocooned" is the course of least resistance, isn't it?) on a regular basis. This gave her something else to look forward to and others to converse with besides the four, now-silent walls of her living room.

What a fantastic idea Elise dreamed up! A few months after her son's death, she began putting together a **Memory Book.** She started from his birth, gathering the birth certifi-  cate, arrival announcement, along with newborn pictures. She wanted to cover all his areas of interest so drove to the school and picked up some memorabilia there. Then his bowling league membership was observed with a copy of one of his score sheets she obtained from the alley.

Of course, she is quick to point out this is not a project you can work on all the time. But on differ- ent days, it felt good to her to be rebuilding a pre- cious life wistfully seen from beginning to abrupt end. It is suggested you involve other family mem- bers, if possible, as they may have a variety of snap- shots to share or letters to contribute, etc. It can be- come a "Family Memory Book." What a super way to remember Mike!

Crystal accidentally hit on a quicker way to find a good day. After crying a lot by herself, she decided to go around her small community and find others who had also lost a spouse. After knocking on doors and introducing herself, both parties would share what had happened to them. It was astounding to realize that every time she started back toward home, she felt so much better. She kept up this activity on a semi-regular basis and firmly believes it is one of the reasons she's still sane today.

Maybe you live in a large city and that idea is not practical. The obvious outgrowth of this suggestion is to check the newspaper for support groups that are meeting. It may be very difficult to show up at the first meeting but I believe once you're there and realize others <u>do</u> hurt like you do . . . you'll not want to miss another meeting. As Lila remarked once in my own support group . . . "At least when I'm here I know everybody else will understand what I'm saying and how I'm feeling. Family and friends may not really 'get it' but it's a relief everyone here sure does."

Maybe your gauge to indicate progress is similar to Dirk's. He remembered that immediately following the news of Darrel's death (at 3 p.m., on Wednesday, the 19th of the month), he was first conscious of 3 p.m. each and every day. Slowly, he arrived at a point where he was just silently observing every Wednesday and the 19th of the month as milestones. After a long time, the milestone became just the 19th. After a couple of years, the 19th of one month slipped by without his noticing.

"I was kind of ashamed of myself," he shared, *"feeling I'd let Darrel down by not acknowledging it, as had been my habit. But then I decided . . . this <u>must</u> be a sign of progress . . . even just a little bit. With that thought in mind, I felt a lot better!"*

Coming Up

As you begin to heal, some of these ideas – and probably other great ones that are "originals" with you – are sure to provide better days for you, now and again.

13

SOMETHING TO THINK ABOUT

SURVIVOR

I learned I was a survivor.
It was in the paper.
His obituary read,
He is survived by his wife, Beverly,
of the home.

I didn't want to survive.
I wanted to die too.
Death had to be easier than surviving

Surviving! I learned to survive.
I survived the sleepless nights,
tortured days, endless weeks,
Holidays, Sundays,
Months of hopelessness.

Survival of the fittest.
I became strong.
Amazingly now, I'm proud
to be a survivor.

I deserve a medal
for the battlescars
– Beverly Romey [1]

Can you easily identify with many of these lines and thoughts? Because feelings change by the day (and the hour!), let me ask it this way ... for **today**, which stanza best describes where you are? Any of the top three are terrifyingly true and seemingly endless, aren't they? I know ... I've been there too.

Oh, to be able to hit the "fast forward" button on the VCR of life to instantly leave that grief treadmill and experience the immense relief, quiet peace and even <u>pride</u> of reaching that last stanza!

Yet even when you arrive there, will you ever be "over it?" The best description of grief's hold on your life is this:

You never get <u>over</u> it;
you just get <u>used</u> to it.

The finality of that sounds so grim at first. But I look at it this way. It doesn't mean you continue to feel that elephant sitting on your chest forever, or the embarrassing memory loss and frustrating lack of concentration always. Those gradually DO improve (thank goodness!) No one stays in that numbness of grief that marked our first days and weeks. But, by losing someone so important and precious you won't be forgetting them either. And after all, you don't WANT to forget them, right? They were a vital part of your life.

So as others wait for you to "get over it" and "get on with life" you will be aware you **will** get used to that special person being away . . . even though the scars of their departure will always be with you. Personally, I don't want to be "over" thinking about and missing Greg. He doesn't deserve to be forgotten. However, I am now "used" to him being away.

It is my hope that having read these pages and found some helpful suggestions to try . . . you'll eventually wake up one day to realize you, too, can announce to the world:

I DID survive!
I AM strong!
I'm ready for my medal!

SPECIAL MESSAGE... to you, the reader. I'm glad you found my book and I want to know if it has been helpful to you. Would you do me a favor? Write and tell me what ideas you read here that have proved most helpful to you.

Also, share with me other creative, unique ways you've found that make this Survival Road journey just a little easier. After all, in learning new ideas, I have the privilege of continually passing them along to other new survivors.

Whatever you'd like to share or information you'd like to receive, I'd be delighted to hear from you! My address is :

P.O. Box 6028
Spokane, WA 99207

Thanks in advance!

Carlene

14

SOURCE NOTES

Urgent!
[1] Grief Sounds I, THEOS Survivors' Outreach Series, pg. 5.

Are You <u>Sure</u> This Is Normal?
[1] Grief Sounds I, THEOS Survivors' Outreach Series, pg. 10.

Hang On To It Or Throw It Out?
[1] Hilarette Brown, Baton Rouge, LA, Days and Seasons of Grief, THEOS Survivors' Outreach Series, pg. 9.

Can't Shut Off The "Water Works!"
[1] Barbara Johnson, <u>So Stick A Geranium In Your Hat And Be Happy</u>, Word Publishing Company, Dallas, pgs. 29 - 30.

Help! That First Year Date Is Coming Up!
[1] Bill Ermatinger, The Compassionate Friends, BEREAVEMENT, November/December 1987, pg. 18.

Something To Think About
[1] Carlene Vester Eneroth, <u>If There's Anything I Can Do . . .</u> Classic Publishing, 1990, pg. 5.

Feel free to use this as an ORDER FORM
or make copies and send them to friends.
Perhaps they are special "survivors" and
need to know they're not alone.

"If There's Anything I Can Do . . . "
or
"Does Anybody Else Hurt This Bad . . .
and Live?"

Copies		Price Each	Total
	"If There's Anything I Can Do . . ."	*$3.95*	
	"Does Anybody Else Hurt This Bad . . ."	*$7.95*	
	Shipping (Number of books ordered times $1.50)		
	Subtotal		
	Washington State Residents add 8% Sales Tax		
	Total Enclosed		

Name _____

Address _____

City _____ State _____ Zip Code _____

Payment must accompany order. Mail to:
Otis Publications, P.O. Box 6028, Spokane, WA 99207
Quantity discounts are available, write for details.